TWO OEDIPAL PLAYS

Two Oedipal Plays

Lenny Cavallaro

Lenny Cavallaro

Two Oedipal Plays:
Hamlet, Revisited
and
Odysseus Acanthoplex
by
Lenny Cavallaro

Dedicated to my children, Maya and Jacob
Copyright 2022 by Lenny Cavallaro

Contents

Preface

Notes to the One-Act Twist on Shakespeare's *Hamlet*

HAMLET, REVISITED: A Familiar Tragedy, but In One Act

Notes on the "Restored" Play

ODYSSEUS ACANTHOPLEX [*Odysseus Wounded By The Spine*]

Preface: What Are These Oedipal Plays – and Why "Closet Drama"?

Neither of these scripts is entirely "original," since both allude to titles that are or were well known. Aristotle discussed *Odysseus Acanthoplex* in his *Poetics*, and it is safe to assume that the work was familiar to his readers, albeit probably less so than *Hamlet* to contemporary theatergoers.

Sophocles is best known for *Oedipus the King*, in which the protagonist discovers — to his horror — that he has slain his father and married his mother. In one guise or another this thematic material is familiar territory for Sophocles; it arises in at least two more of his dramas, including *Odysseus Acanthoplex*.

In *The Interpretation of Dreams* Freud explains that Hamlet is unable to avenge his father's murder because of his repressed Oedipus complex — i.e., because Claudius has killed Hamlet's father and now sleeps with Hamlet's mother, and thus "shows him [i.e., Hamlet] the repressed wishes of childhood realized." However, we know that Hamlet will ultimately slay his [step-]father. Moreover, in Act III, scene iv Hamlet explicitly instructs his mother not to sleep with the King: suggestively Oedipal material,to say the least.

I have written a very short, one-act *Hamlet*, and I have attempted a conjectural "restoration" of *Odysseus Acanthoplex*. In both texts we encounter similar thematic motifs, and while the works are vastly different, I feel the pairing is indeed coherent.

* * *

"Closet Drama" is applied to a play that is probably better suited for a "reading" – most often, by just a single reader – than an on-stage production. Such works have enriched our Western cultural heritage, arguably beginning as early as the *Dialogues* of Plato. In the 19th century closet dramas were often written in verse, and both parts of Goethe's immortal *Faust* may have been intended for reading rather than stage.

Closet dramas ultimately give rise to a related form, the "closet screenplay," which is also intended to be read aloud (again by a solitary reader). The "script" within Aldous Huxley's *Ape and Essence* stands as a noteworthy representative of this genre.

At length we come to "readers theater," which is sometimes offered with a dubious apostrophe. This term refers to the presentation by multiple actors of a script that, again, is not intended for actual production. The players generally sit in chairs and read their lines, rather than act.

What, then, is the one-act version of *Hamlet*? Is it a closet drama or a work for "readers theater"? Could it stand as either, and perhaps even withstand direction on the stage?

The answers to all of these questions are the same: yes. However, I prefer to stay with "closet drama," and then to modify the term to allow more than one reader. Moreover, my rendition of *Hamlet* includes a number of non-speaking parts, which might be realized far more effectively by actors engaged on a stage than mute "readers" seated in chairs. Finally, a work intended for "readers theater" appears to preclude the possibility of an actual production, whereas a closet drama might more reasonably lend itself to that artistic medium.

From a practical standpoint, my *Hamlet* is a one-act drama, perhaps as brief as five or six minutes in duration (though conceivably longer), yet it requires six "actors" (two of whom have non-speaking roles), as well as a handful of soldiers. Upon reflection, I cheerfully concede the difficulties presented for so short a production – at least under normal circumstances.

And how of *Odysseus Acanthoplex*? The restored play is barely one-third the length of *Oedipus the King*. Moreover, with five characters plus the Chorus and the Lords of Ithaca, a bizarre stage (effectively two settings, rather than the customary one), and the abbreviated duration, this text may inevitably present similar challenges. Nevertheless, I believe it actually *could* work, although only within a production of several "short" plays.

For now, however, closet drama seems an apt description for both texts. Be that as it may, I hope the reader can imagine the following as truly dramatic works.

HAMLET, REVISITED: A Familiar Tragedy, But In One Act
by
Lenny Cavallaro

Notes to the One-Act Twist on Shakespeare's *Hamlet*

As dearly as we may love the bard, there is no reason we cannot reconsider his plots. What I have proposed for this one-act effort is a somewhat different presentation that draws upon the following:

1. Is Claudius guilty? Hamlet and the Ghost inform us that his uncle has murdered his own brother (i.e., Hamlet's father), to gain both the throne and the Queen. I am not the first to wonder whether Shakespeare perhaps tells us somewhat too early who the murderer is. Moreover, his version of events overlooks the fact that Hamlet, an adult son (cf., "Alas, poor Yorick" for his age!), would surely have been declared King; his uncle had no claim at all.
2. The tale of Hamlet seems to at least some extent derived from Greek mythology. If we look at the tragedies of both Oedipus (murder of the father; marriage to the mother) and Agamemnon (Orestes driven to murder his mother and uncle – her second husband – to avenge his father), we can consider Hamlet in an intriguing light.
3. Given these literary and psychological roots, let us reflect upon the possibility that Hamlet actually *is* mad. Suppose the real tragedy is that he has an Oedipal fixation on his mother; that he has apparently been driven "over the edge" by her remarriage; suppose – melding the familiar Freudian imagery with Jungian projection – that, as we shall learn at the very end, it is actually *Hamlet* who has (accidentally?) killed his own father, though he sincerely believes his uncle is to blame. The tragedy now takes on a totally different dimension.

4. Each time someone has stumbled upon the truth (e.g., Polonius, Rosencrantz, Guildenstern), he has apparently come to an untimely end.
5. In a secondary thematic twist, Hamlet and Ophelia have consummated their love. The unexpected pregnancy has driven the guilt-ridden Ophelia to suicide and prompts a cold-blooded, calculating Claudius and vengeful Laertes to destroy the person responsible.
6. Claudius is almost blameless until the very end. To preserve the kingdom, he has reluctantly accepted the title of King; political forces have subsequently pressured him into marriage. After the unruly Hamlet threatens both the stability of Denmark and the safety of the royal family, Claudius casts his lot with Laertes, determined to rid the court of his madcap nephew. The latter's skill with the sword again leaves the stage littered with corpses, but at the end, to Horatio's (and everyone's) surprise, Hamlet confesses to killing his own father.

The language is predominantly in iambic pentameter, save where it is in prose. [Shakespeare wrote large chunks of his text, including the "Alas, poor Yorick" lines, in prose.] Like the Bard himself, I occasionally interpolate a line in hexameter (12 syllables).

One note about the delivery: Polonius is sometimes read in three syllables and sometimes in four.

With this preface behind us, the one-act piece is now respectfully submitted for reading – though probably not viewing – pleasure!

HAMLET, REVISITED

DRAMATIS PERSONAE

FORTINBRAS – Prince of Norway, and effectively ruler of Denmark
HORATIO – friend of the late Prince Hamlet
HAMLET – Prince of Denmark
CLOWN – one of the grave-diggers
OPHELIA – sister of Laertes
LAERTES – brother of Ophelia
SOLDIERS – attendant upon Fortinbras

HAMLET, REVISITED

[FORTINBRAS *is seated.* SOLDIERS *bring in* HORATIO *for questioning. As the latter speaks,* HAMLET *appears in the foreground, where he will offer comments about the narration.*]

[*In the background,* SOLDIERS *are seen carrying several* CORPSES, *one at a time, off stage. One of the bodies is that of a woman. Two are those of men.*]

FORT: How came this noble prince to such sad end
And all the House of Denmark thus to lie
Cold corpses, slain by sword or poison'd wine?
And these are not the only deaths of late.
From all accounts, there have been others ta'en,
Cut down by means unnatural and most foul.
Come, Sir, explain, for I would hear it all.
HOR.: My noble Lord. The King here slain thou knowst –
'Tis Claudius, the brother of that King
That laid low Norway when the King thine uncle
Against us thrust his might. That first, whose name
Was Hamlet, like his son's, fell to his death.
Until this day, we thought it was ill luck,
An accident that cost that lord his life.
Oh, Sir – It was not so! And this sad tale
Begins far earlier, with his wife, the Queen.
For she, who loved her husband for a time
Gave birth and ever after loved her son
Yet more. Indeed, it was as if she had
Ta'en him into her heart, if not her bed.
She doted on the boy, and he on her.

And none of us saw anything amiss
Or worse, unnatural, although I must
Confess that in our teens, I thought my Prince,
Lord Hamlet, was at times too close to her,
And too far from his Sire.
[FORTINBRAS *and some of his* SOLDIERS *seem amused, while* HAMLET *seems offended, and hurls an angry glance across the stage.*]
FORT: What Greek myth
Is this that thou wouldst share? I'm not unschooled,
And know full well of Oedipus and all
That fell at Thebes. But if there's more to say
About this family's woe, please do continue.
HOR.: Lord Hamlet was (*hesitant*) insane. Thou mayst have heard
How oft his wits betrayed him. We all knew;
These things were widely known, and known by all.
But what we did not see – alas the day –
Was just how mad, how ill, how sick he was.
Until his dying moments, in my arms, I lived
In ignorance of all that had transpired.
FORT: Come, come. Let's have it all! Let's have it all!
HOR.: (*reluctantly*) I'll ask a question. Answer an thou canst:
Upon the death of sovereign, who rules next –
His issue, son and heir, or wife's consort
As, in this case, the older Hamlet's brother?
FORT: A fool could answer this one, Sir: the son
Being of age must now assume the throne.
HOR: Indeed! Then answer this, an' if thou canst:
How came't Hamlet, agèd twenty-eight
Did bear the title, "Prince," whilst 'pon the throne
His uncle sat, now wedded to the Queen?
FORT: (*puzzled*) A mystery, that's one I cannot solve.
HOR: It was a ruling forced upon this House
By all the lords. Prince Hamlet was insane

And with his father's death his melancholy
Worsened. Clearly, he could in no way
Be trusted with the reins of power, so:
The Council ordered Claudius to ascend,
And in Levirate custom take the Queen
As wife. This show, they thought would in its way
Legitimize the reign of loathèd Claudius,
Who by all rights had no claim on the throne.
[*In the background, enter the* CLOWN, *holding a skull in his hands. He tosses the skull to* HAMLET.]

HAM [*aside, to audience, after studying the skull and then tossing it back.* CLOWN *exits.*]:
Are you surprised to learn I am so old?
Why I can ev'n remember poor old Yorick –
He who hath lain in the grave some three-and-twenty years.
Alas, poor Yorick! I knew him, Horatio: a fellow
of infinite jest, of most excellent fancy: he hath
borne me on his back a thousand times.
HOR: But lo, this marriage gave my friend the Prince
No respite from his ravings. Nay, instead
It drove him deeper into madness and
Some said, resentment of the King, his uncle.
FOR: I knew the man, Horatio. He was fair
Though never to be crossed, and yet I thought
He loved his nephew dearly – so it seemed.
HOR: He also loved his wife, and this, indeed,
Did threaten her mad son, my friend the Prince.
But didst thou know some others from our court –
Polonius, Guildenstern, and Rosenkrantz?
FOR: By name, alone, though else I knew them not.
HOR: Nor ever shall, for all are slain!
FOR: By whom?
HOR: That same Prince Hamlet, who now lies in death

Himself laid low, by treachery of the King.
FOR: So I have heard. Then Claudius, otherwise
So noble of intent, so loyal and true,
Did with Laertes hatch a plot so vile
That all three now do lie in death along
With Gertrude, Queen and wife, and Hamlet's mother?
HOR: This thou tell'st true. King Claudius, though loathe
To strike at Hamlet was by that mad Prince
Provoked beyond belief. The latter staged
A play through which to make the court believe
That Claudius had slain the erstwhile King.
HAMLET (*aside, chuckling*): Yes, that was quite a coup!
The players served me nobly! Ah, how they got under
Mine uncle's skin. Truly, the play's the thing
With which to crush the gonads of the King!
HOR: And when he slew Polonius, there were riots!
The vulgar in the streets cried out for justice.
And Laertes, old Polonius' son,
Sought vengeance. And still worse was yet to come.
FOR: How so?
HOR: The fair Ophelia, daughter of the slain
And sister to Laertes, now herself succumbed
To madness. So we thought. Also, alas –
HAM: The sickness did betray her. Yes, she was
With child, and it was mine. Well – accidents happen,
E'en in the most dysfunctional families!
[*Enter* OPHELIA. HAMLET *looks upon her tenderly.*]
Yet I did love her ...
[*Exit* OPHELIA, *who stands off to the side.*]
HOR: She was ruined. Dishonored, and for sure
No more a virgin, she now stood disgraced.
And jumped into the pond, where she soon drowned.
HAM: I loved her, truly. Of that death, did I

Repent, and thus leapt into her cold grave,
To be assaulted by her madman brother,
Whom I most truly did not love at all.
HOR: Now came the news from England, Hamlet had
By dint of stolen seals two noble lords
Fair Guildenstern and Rosenkrantz deliver'd
Unto their deaths. These two made four – the girl,
Her father and that pair – with threats upon
The King himself. It was too much for Claudius
To endure. And thus he took unto his trust
Laertes, and their plot unhatched. For sport,
Prince Hamlet would Ophelia's brother match
His skill at fencing, whilst unknown to him –
HAM: Unknown to me, that pair contrived my death.
i' faith, the plan was clever. I picked my sword,
[*He pulls out a fencing foil. Enter* LAERTES.]
While Laertes chose his – a tool whose tip
Was sharp, unblunted, like my own.
[*Laertes selects his own weapon. They begin to fence. Hamlet scores a hit.*]
That blade
Had poison 'pon it.
[*More fencing. Again, Hamlet scores a hit.*]
And, in case his skills
Were not up to the task, they had devised
Refreshment for me – one fine bowl of wine
Into which they had mixed more pois'n. But Mother
Drank the wine, and swooned. Meanwhile, distracted,
I let Laertes scratch me. And at once
[LAERTES *sticks his blade in* HAMLET's *arm.*]
I saw his blade was real. That instant I
Disarm'd him, ...

[HAMLET's *sudden response knocks the blade out of* LAERTES' *hand. He holds off his foe, picks up the lethal weapon, hands his blunted foil to* LAERTES, *and proceeds to fence with him.*]

grabbed the blade, and ran him through. [LAERTES *falls.*]
But as he fell ...
HOR: But as he fell, Laertes did confess
The plot and Hamlet's imminent demise.
At once, the Prince upon the King did spring,
And sent him to his death. This much you know.
FORT: So I have heard, and do in part believe.
Yet I suspect there's more you have to tell.
HOR: Indeed, my Lord, and with your patience ending,
I'll soon conclude, for here this tale hath ending.
The prince died in my arms, and ere he died,
He told me something more – a truth which I
Must now reveal. His mother, Gertrude, Queen –
[FORTINBRAS *and* HORATIO *are almost frozen in place.* HAMLET *continues, while struggling for life. He is mortally wounded.*]

HAM: Enough! 'Tis time! Let us tell all. Mine uncle,
That incestuous beast, did wed her, and she
Took him into her bed! – the bed my father,
Her late husband, called his own! What a falling off
was there! But much worse still, I soon believed
That in her advanced age nevertheless
She did conceive a child!
Father, himself, she had kept at a distance;
And it was just. For her affections fell
Upon not him, but me! And in my madness,
I perceived my father as my foe.
My mind is clouded now. And why I blamed
A blameless Uncle, I know not, although
There was a time, Lord knows, I truly thought
That *he, not I, had slain the King.* But nay!

My father never slipped over the ledge.
'Twas *I, in fact*, who pushed him thence – methinks
An accident, though who on earth can tell?
And I talked to myself at times, whilst through
These halls a-stumbling went and yet,
'Twas rare that someone heard me. Polonius?
Now, he once got too close, and when he cried
Out in alarm, I stuck my blade inside
Him. All cries ceased, and that crass, meddling fool
Departed on his way most quickly to
A convocation of politic worms!
Rosencrantz and Guildenstern heard me talking
In my sleep. 'Twas they who recommended
The exile off in England, where my madness
Would go unnoticed. Yet with stolen seal,
I had them slain, on orders of the King!
About Ophelia: truly I repent. We spoke
Of country matters, yet she knew the truth,
And was convinced that I belonged in Hell.
And said she'd sooner bear a child that might
Be Satan's.
[*Enter* OPHELIA.]
OPH: Better with vile Judas, or a Cain
Inside my womb, than seed from him, the man
Who slew my father, thrice accursed wretch!
[*Exit* OPHELIA.]
Thus Laertes, upon her death contrived
With Claudius to destroy my life and had
My mother not their second victim been
We justly had for their success now prayed.
[HAMLET *falls.* HORATIO *rushes over to hold him, until he dies.*]
Now have I one more death upon my soul,
My mother joined an uncle otherwise

Full innocent of any crime, and with
These words, Horatio, I'm off to Hell.
[HAMLET *dies as* Horatio *speaks.*]
HOR: Good night, sweet Prince! For thine eternal rest
Leave it to Him that judges last and best.
Thy crimes confessed, thy struggles here do cease
With Madness, that hast ta'en from thee all peace.
Thy damaged wits, alone, destroyed thy love
So pray God show you mercy and peace Above!
[*Drums sound a funeral march beat. The* SOLDIERS *carry* HAMLET *off stage. Curtain falls.*]

FINIS

ODYSSEUS ACANTHOPLEX [Odysseus Wounded By The Spine]
The conjectural "restoration" of a drama by Sophocles
by
Lenny Cavallaro

Notes on the "Restored" Play

This restoration, drawn from various accounts of the myth and the few remaining fragments of a "lost" drama by Sophocles, is designed primarily to present the story. Odysseus has returned to Ithaca, having gone off in an effort to appease Poseidon. While at Dodona, he has visited the oracle of Zeus, who shared a fatal vision: Odysseus will be slain by his son!

In his *Poetics* Aristotle wrote about *hamartia*, the fatal flaw that causes the tragic character to "miss the mark." This hamartia most often manifests as hubris, and in a culture as fatalistic as that of the ancient Greeks, an attempt to escape one's fate – i.e., to pit one's mortal wits against those of one or more gods or goddesses – was deemed extraordinarily hubristic. Indeed, the "sin" of Oedipus (Sophocles' best-known tragic hero) was not that he killed his father and married his mother, but the hubris he showed when he fled Corinth (and his presumed parents) in response to the oracle's warning of his impending doom.

The prideful Odysseus also succumbs to hubris. He attempts to evade what the gods have decreed, and to this end he exiles his son, Telemachus.

The hero is unaware that he has another son.* On the long journey back from Troy, Odysseus had spent a year (or more) on the island of Kirke, a goddess who initially behaved more like a witch. Kirke bore Odysseus a son, whom she named Telegonus.

Greek myths conveniently overlook such details as chronology. Even if it took Odysseus seven more years to return to Ithaca (most of which he spent as the captive of another goddess, Calypso), and perhaps some additional months to kill the suitors, restore the throne, and depart again (carrying an oar) to offer penance to Poseidon, his second son ought not have been much more than seven years of age.

How strange indeed that this Telegonus was already a grown man, and stranger still that at the end of the original drama, he would marry Penelope!

It is obvious that Freud was unaware of *Odysseus Acanthoplex,* and probably also of *The Trachiniae* (*The Women of Trachis*), yet another powerful drama by Sophocles. At the conclusion of the latter play, Herakles (Hercules) orders his son, Hyllus, to burn him alive (by setting the funeral pyre alight) and also to marry Herakles' mistress, Iole. Thus, in the Oedipal sense, Hyllus must kill his father and marry a woman who has earlier lain with his father. [Odysseus alludes to this story in the present drama.]

In *Odysseus Acanthoplex,* Sophocles probably drew upon a version of the myths presented in the *Telegony* of Eugammon, which is also "lost." The latter took this suggestive motif even further. Telegonus does indeed slay Odysseus (accidentally). He then brings Penelope and Telemachus back to Aeaea, where Kirke makes all three immortal, whereupon Telemachus marries Kirke (his father's mistress) and Telegonus marries Penelope (his father's wife, though not his biological mother).

A study of the Greek obsession with the theme (i.e., killing the father, marrying the mother) lies outside the focus of this effort. Suffice it to say that I am far from convinced Freud interpreted *Oedipus Rex* correctly. The case can certainly (and no less reasonably) be made that the ancient Greeks may have intuitively grasped a concept that came to public awareness only in the latter half of the last century: that men and women peak sexually at different ages, separated by approximately one generation. Thus, Oedipus (perhaps late teens) may have been in his sexual prime, even as Jocasta began hers.

That argument aside, I prefer instead to view this present drama as another study of hamartia, manifested as the hero's hubris, and indeed we see (as Homer taught us) that "feeble are the wits of men, when paired 'gainst those of gods." We certainly noted the hubris of Odysseus in the *Odyssey,* when he mocked Polyphemus and told him that it was he (i.e., Odysseus) who had outsmarted and blinded him. In this drama, the hero waxes hubristic again when he exiles Telemachus in an effort to outwit his fate. Finally, he attacks Telegonus, assuming that he cannot be slain by anyone other than Telemachus. He is humbled yet further in his dying agonies when he realizes the ultimate ironic twist: that the spine of the stingray, one of Poseidon's sea creatures, has brought him to his doom. [Tiresias had prophesied (in *The Odyssey*) that the hero's death would come "out of the sea."]

Of course, it is quite possible that Sophocles' drama concluded with the "happy ending" and double wedding after the death of Odysseus. Accordingly, in this rendition, I let the Chorus suggest that somewhat Oedipal outcome. However, Kirke returns in the Exodos and rejects the notion – apparently because she had truly loved Odysseus and would not make a mockery of his death.

If this reconstruction were for stage (and not "closet drama" or "readers theater"), I would ideally envision a Chorus of sixteen, rather than the traditional fifteen of Sophocles. They would be broken into balanced groups of four or eight and speak as one voice. The Leader (presumably in Group One) has a number of solo lines, a practice also seen in the original.

Of course, the Chorus enter with the Parados, and it would be inappropriate to have them onstage during the Prologue. Thus, the *dramatis personae* includes the "Lords of Ithaca," who need not number more than four. Similarly, a Chorus of four could suffice admirably.

I decided to write much of the drama in a somewhat compromised iambic pentameter – admittedly a rather unusual choice, and clearly not a pattern drawn from the Greek tragedians. My decision was strongly influenced by Gilbert Murray's wonderful translation of *Iphigenia in Tauris* (1911). That brilliant scholar not only set most of Euripides' text in iambic pentameter, but actually contrived to work rhymes into large portions of the drama. I also hasten to append the oft-quoted remark of Robert Frost: "There are only two meters in English, strict and loose iambic." While no one ever questioned the extensive use of iambic pentameter in my *Hamlet, Revisited: A Familiar Tragedy, But In One Act*, I suspect it may raise an eyebrow with a Greek tragedy. Nevertheless, I consider that meter altogether appropriate, notwithstanding the havoc invariably wrought by the names of certain characters and the three-syllable pronunciation of Ithaca!

I must therefore offer a brief explanation about the sections *not* written in iambic pentameter. These begin in Episode 3, after the mortally wounded hero has been carried back to the palace: My daughter, Maya Cara Wax Cavallaro, noted that perhaps when Odysseus is poisoned and dying, he is in an altered state, and this in turn invites an altered meter. Another interpretation is that as he becomes aware of his mortality – and later his hubris – the process affects his meter. The less structured lines effectively reflect a shift in Odysseus, and to some extent his impending death may even influence the way the others speak as well.

The language itself is somewhat archaic, and deliberately so. However, I use "thee," "thine," "thou," and "thy" only when a god or goddess speaks to a mortal. The language is at times also mildly Homeric. The repetitions, both Homeric and non-Homeric (e.g., "the wine-dark seas") are thus intentional.

I follow the structure of the Greek tragedy – i.e., the Prologue, Parados, a set of three Episodes and Stasimons, and the concluding Exodos – quite intentionally. This is my *hommage à Sophocles.* In an obvious *hommage à Shakespeare,* I conclude each section with rhymed couplets.

Those few fragments of the original tragedy appear in the Prologue in italics and bold typeface, although they might instead be set in another font, size, or even color. I have set these in iambic pentameter and may thus claim credit for the ensuing "translation." I trust the damage is minimal! More to the point, though, I hope readers will gain yet greater appreciation for the genius of Sophocles. We can but wonder at how marvelously he must have told the same tale.

---

*Some versions of the Odysseus saga mentioned his post-*Odyssey* relationship with Kallidike queen of the Thesprotians, who bore him a son, Polypoites. Other works speak of yet additional progeny of both genders. In this play Kirke alludes to this third son (and future king).

ODYSSEUS ACANTHOPLEX
[Odysseus Wounded by the Spine]
DRAMATIS PERSONAE

Odysseus, King of Ithaca

Lords of Ithaca (4 or more in number)

Telemachus, son of Odysseus and Penelope

Penelope, Queen of Ithaca

The Chorus (4 to 16 citizens of Ithaca), including the Leader

Kirke, a goddess and enchantress on whose island Odysseus stayed one year

Telegonus, son of Odysseus and Kirke

The STAGE reflects the typically sparse Greek theater. The palace of Odysseus and Penelope in Ithaca is to the rear and swung slightly to the right. To the far right, in front of the palace, is a small wall (or perhaps merely a screen), behind which the CHORUS may retreat as necessary, though they will remain visible. To the far left is a smaller area, set off to represent the palace of KIRKE at Aeaea.

PROLOGUE

ODYSSEUS, PENELOPE, TELEMACHUS, and some LORDS of Ithaca.

ODYSSEUS: Once more have I these precious shores departed
And yet again have I returned to you
My friends and family, and loyal subjects.
Athena's fav'rite, here I humbly stand
To face your questions, and to share my tale
Or at the least, some vital parts thereof.

LORDS: Hail, long-tried royal Odysseus, our King
And welcome back to these Ithacan shores!

ODYSSEUS: Return is sweet, but welcome sweeter still!

LORDS: Whence have you come? Pray tell us all about
Th'adventures of these latest trav'ls 'pon
The wine-dark seas. Where have you been, and what
Became of that long oar with which you left?
ODYSSEUS: I beg for patience. When I last did speak
With bless'd Tiresias, he told me plain:
"You must go forth, and carry thence an oar
Until you have such people found that they
Know not the sea. Then when some person there
Shall claim you carry on that tired back
A fan for winnowing, you shall be sure
The place is reached whereat you must your penance
Provide unto the Lord and god, Poseidon."
This was no easy task, yet I persevered
Until some fellow asked, "**Whence comes the gift**
You have upon your mighty shoulders? It
Does seem a fan for winnowing indeed!"
His words, exact, and thus I knew where I
Some sacrifice would make to 'pease the god
Whom I offended on my journey home
From war at Troy. Yet on the way I'd heard
That Zeus was living at nearby Dodona
Whom mortals call Zeus of the sacred temple
And where I might obtain some guidance from
The prophesying priestess serving him.
And there I went, and waited for a time,
Unsure: *perhaps someone would venture out,*
But if she would not, still no one from there,
From Dodona, or from the hollows of
Great Pytho [i.e., Delphi] *could persuade me even so*
To put a stop to praises of the god
At great Dodona. Thus, at length, did come

Forth from the cave the priestess herself
And from her blessed lips came out the words
That bring me back to these Ithacan lands
Whereon I rule. "Hail, Son of Laertes,
And Lord of Ithaca," she sang, then paused.
"The favored of Athena, and proud scion
Of Hermes fleet-of-foot. Heedst thou these words:
Thou shalt thy destiny confront ere long,
By death not from a stranger, but from him
Who sprang forth from thy loins: This is thy doom,
Thou shalt be slain by thine own noble son!"
    [*Everyone cries out in alarm at this news.*]
Thus I return, and must my fate address.
The oracle of Zeus himself decrees
That this, my son, brave Telemachus here
Whom I have trusted with my very life
Would that same life cut down.
One of the LORDS: It cannot be!
Think back, my King, upon most recent strife
Wherein he saved your life 'pon three occasions
As you both fought so bravely to regain
Your palace from the men who would be king
And husband to Penelope. Without
Your noble son, you surely would have fallen,
Outnumbered as you were in mortal trial!
TELEMACHUS: I must append my love and strong devotion
For I have ever proved a loyal son.
ODYSSEUS: I hear you both, and in your words, there's truth
Yet blindness, too. We mortal men cannot
Divine the message from the gods above
In perfect form. I think Telemachus
Would sooner cut his hand from off his arm
Than harm me with it, yet I would take care

For accidents may fall upon us and
Most surely bring us to our ruin. So,
I cannot treat my son as a usurper.
Nor can I see him as a deadly foe,
Yet I am sure that while he lives, my life
In some grave danger lies. Thus I've contrived
Expedient for the good of one and all.
LORDS: But how can you escape the god's decree?
ODYSSEUS: I wouldn't presume –
PENELOPE: And yet, that's what you do!
Great King and noble husband, please reflect.
The Fates are goddesses; the voice you heard
Was from the mouth of Zeus himself. What's more,
We are well taught that feeble are the wits
Of men when matched 'gainst those of the divine!
And though I've loved you all these years despite
Long absence, yet I must beg to observe
It was your own strong pride when you had blinded
Vile Polyphemus that upon your crew
Wrought havoc and the deaths of one and all.
ODYSSEUS: For which I did repent and to that end
Made penitence unto his sire, Poseidon.
Now, hear me well, and learn what I intend.
I do survive, as all know well, despite
Outrageous odds. When on the windy plains
Of ruined Troy great Hector and his forces
Nearly took our measure on the field:
When arrows flew, and javelins came my way;
When deadly sword thrusts tried me, yet somehow
I found a way to live. When Polyphemus
Trapped us in his cave, we were quite doomed,
Yet once again, I found a way to live.
One hundred eight vile suitors we opposed,
The four of us – my son, and Eumaeus,

And brave Philoteus – yet we prevailed.
Should I these triumphs now forget and like
A coward, sit and wait not just for death,
But for the ruination of my son
Condemned for patricide, and cursed by all?
This I cannot, and thus I have my plan.
Telemachus: I shall myself be pilot
To vessels sailed to that desolate isle
Where you shall exile on the rocky crags.
Its shelter is secure, and we'll provide
Such food and clothing as you may require.
Meanwhile, we must seek out another voice
To learn for sure the Oracle was correct.
Perhaps in time, I'll die some other way,
Or being close to death, can call you back
That we may part in peace and loving bond.
You will remain my son and heir; meanwhile
This is my plan, the safest course to take.
TELEMACHUS: I shall obey, as always, my wise father,
And bless the happy day of my return!
PENELOPE: This plan seems sound, although I like it not.
Yet still, I cannot offer you another.
ODYSSEUS: I'll to the docks. My ship will be the first.
Take you the next, and we'll await the worst.
> *Exeunt Odysseus, Penelope, Telemachus, and Lords to the Palace*

PARADOS

Enter the CHORUS, chanting:
[First Four]: What news is this we hear of our great King
Whose house now seems asunder. Can it be
That rumors are proved right?
[Second Four] His royal son
Great Telemachus, noble and so true
Who saved his father's life not once, but thrice
In battle for their home and kingdom: he

Is to the rocky crag in exile sent
Where 'pon the sea he can look out in all
Directions, never finding any hope
To 'scape the sentence placed upon him by
His father. What can ail Laertes' son
That he this sentence 'pon the boy has cast:
He leaves the palace till some unknown time
When his return may be considered due?
[Third Four] Although I dearly love my king – I swear –
I still cannot agree with this, his plan.
For never was there truer loving son
Than his, who loved his father more than all.
[Fourth Four] They claim the Oracle has had her say
And from the lips of mighty Zeus does teach
Our king that he shall die quite slain by him
He has begot.
CHORUS [all]: And thus this sentence fell
And Telemachus bade us all farewell.

The Chorus remain on stage, but fall back behind the screen.

EPISODE ONE

Enter KIRKE and TELEGONUS
KIRKE: The grey-eyed daughter of all-mighty Zeus [i.e., Athena]
Has answered thy request for information
Thou wouldst of him seek knowledge, and 'tis fair
I should impart it, seeking all the while
To shelter thee, my only son, from harm.
That said, once more I must oppose thy will
Oft stated to seek out thy lord and sire
Who knows not of thy birth. Odysseus,
Ithaca's lord and king, would be most proud
To see the noble specimen his son
Hath now become. Still, I must ask of thee
Some reason: how canst thou now justify
This mission. He can never offer thee

The love a father ought have given to
A son conceived in love. You'll meet as men;
No less; no more. Yes, had he known the love
I've shown thee from thine earliest breaths, I'm sure
A father true he would have been. But now
He's missed the chance, as with the other
Telemachus, the son borne by his wife,
Penelope. And yes, it is now told,
A third son from that hero's loins will rule
As the Thesprotian king, yet of ye three,
Odysseus knows of but one, thy brother
The noble Telemachus. Thus, I ask
And ask yet once again, what is the madness
That drives thee to chance all upon the seas
Of great Poseidon, Lord of the watery realms?
And even if thou shouldst ill fate evade
And find harsh weather aimed not at thy boat,
Who knows what savage breed of men thou mayst
Encounter?
TELEGONUS: Shall I fear to face some foe
Unnamed, and cower like a frightened child
Behind his mother's arms? Nay, I cannot
Ignore the need to satisfy desire
To know my sire. As for your other dread,
Fear not. I am most skilled with weapons forged
Of fire! Nay, Mother, I shall not abide
With you forever, cringing like a coward
Because some day, in place unknown some villain
May fall upon me, with his icy blade.
As for the reservations you pronounced,
I ask you to reflect upon your motives:
Is it my safety, or perhaps some poor,
Misguided fear of her, Penelope,
His wife, to whom the hero hath returned.

What folly this! A goddess – you – cannot
A mortal envy!
KIRKE: As I surely don't.
Nor have I aught but love for his poor wife,
Whom he doth love far more than me, I'll say it.
TELEGONUS: Let it be so! And give me now your blessings.
My ship is ready, with a loyal crew
To row to Ithaca, I must away
To meet my father. 'Tis my destiny.
KIRKE: Brave son! I know thy mind is quite made up,
And this, thy course is set. Yet let me now
Provide thee with some help: Behold this spear!
Hephaestus hath designed it, at my prompting
And made a weapon supernatural.
Whilst in thine hands, no man can ever slay thee.
Behold this deadly spine within the shaft.
Poseidon, he himself, hath granted us
A sting-ray's spine, full venomous, from which
The slightest scratch shall bring the agony
Of painful death. So if thou must depart
I beg thee take this gift, a mother's boon.
And I shall rest assured thou wilt come back.
TELEGONUS: For which I thank you. Now, you must reflect:
Poseidon doth his favor grant, yet still
You have such fear of ill to come my way
Upon the wine-dark seas? This makes no sense!
And if no foe shall slay me on the field,
The journey is quite safe. So now I yearn
To leave, to meet my sire, and return.

Exeunt Kirke and Telegonus

The Chorus emerge from behind the screen.

STASIMON ONE

CHORUS [First Four] Our king, Odysseus, has here returned
Good news for us in this our native soil

Yet his arrival is not all the news
That we have heard.
[Second Four] A stranger has descended
Upon these shores. Whence has he come, and why?
What brings him here? How came he 'cross the seas,
And how? Alone, or one of many men?
[Third Four] I hear he is alone, and by the laws
Of hospitality, we should receive
Him, even as our Lord Odysseus
Was nobly treated on the island shores
Of Alkinous, King of all the Phaiacians
Who brought him back to us.
[Fourth Four] Alas, I fear
You have not heard the news. Some foolish men
Our own Ithacans, true, yet surely fools,
Attacked and gave him battle.
[Third Four] And prevailed?
[Fourth Four] Not so! This hero proved too strong for them
And in a trice they were by him all slain.
CHORUS [all]: A crisis for our king has thus arisen.
And he, alone, is suited to this task.
What he will do we shall soon learn. Till then,
We pray the stranger does not kill again.

EPISODE TWO

Enter ODYSSEUS, in armor, holding his helmet

ODYSSEUS: I hear the wagging tongues of those who hold
Each rumor, as 'tis borne, as something sacred,
A gift from the Olympian gods above.
And from this babble I cannot discern
A solid tale. Come, some of you and speak:
What has transpired here while I was gone?
LEADER: Great King! I fear it is somewhat ... unclear!
ODYSSEUS (becoming angry): Unclear? Is this the answer to your king?

I am but hours gone, and all's "unclear"?
We rowed my son Telemachus to safety
    Upon the nearby isolated rock
    Of which I spoke. He is full well supplied:
    Well clothed, well stocked with food, and to that hut --
    A stony, modest place, yet 'twill suffice
    To keep him sheltered – there did he retire.
    We then rowed home, and saw nor ship nor sign
    Of some invasion, yet I could not walk
    Ten paces on my native soil before
    Confused reports assailed me from all sides.
LEADER: My Lord. It seems some battle has begun.
ODYSSEUS: What army dares to challenge us at arms?
What strength, what numbers are this brazen foe?
LEADER: Our best reports would say no force, save one
A single foe, a stranger, and alone.
ODYSSEUS: A single foe! But is he man or god?
LEADER: A mortal, sure, for thus he did arrive:
With just a spear, and holding to a board,
Half-drowned, and coughing water from his lungs.
This information is the best I've heard.
All else is gossip, from the mouths of fools.
ODYSSEUS: How came the violence, then, from one half-drowned?
Did he attack, or did we all forget
The debts we owe a guest?
CHORUS [First Four] Some say the men
From Ithaca drew weapons first and paid
The greatest price.
CHORUS [Second Four] Yet other voices swear
'Twas he whose weapon was to blame.
CHORUS [Third Four] And I
Have yet another wrinkle to the tale.
CHORUS [Fourth Four] A man was slain, an Ithacan, by him
Who from the sea emerged.

CHORUS [all] And thus his friends
Confronted him who stood thereof accused.
Enter PENELOPE
ODYSSEUS: Enough! This is unfortunate, and yet
In fairness I suspect the tale is muddled
A man half-drowned already slew another,
Yet no one saw him leave the shore? Perhaps,
Though most unlikely. Ne'ertheless, I must
Investigate. And if the stranger can
Convince me with his words that he'd no part
In that offense, he stands forgiv'n for all
He did in self-defense when they attacked,
And shall as guest be welcomed at my home,
And treated royally. Yet rest assured
That should this man convince me not, or choose
To try his luck with weapons, he'll soon find
Odysseus remains what he has been:
Athena's favorite and swift Hermes' kin.
PENELOPE: Brave husband, please forbear! And heed the wife
Who saw you off to war at Troy, and then
Heard naught, while you did wander on the seas
As many years again. A woman's fears
Are oft ignored; we know this is the case.
Yet have I not looked out with heavy heart
Grown fearful far too often as I wept
And prayed you would return unharmed?
How many times must you take up your arms?
Why now, when younger men can take the challenge
And prove themselves most worthy to assume
The right to call themselves Ithacans?
And if this stranger comes in peace, let them
Unto our palace guide him. If instead,
He comes to slay, what can one man alone
Achieve, opposed by one and all? Nay stay:

Confront him not, whoever he may be,
For your sake, and my own, and Ithaca's.
ODYSSEUS (sarcastically): Good wife, what dreams and portents have you had?
What seers have you consulted who advised
You thus? Behold! I am Odysseus,
Still living, hale and hearty, and quite strong.
PENELOPE: I claim no dreams, nor seers, nor other forms
Of divination can support this fear.
Most dreadful in its weight. I beg you stay.
It is the feeling, which has seized my heart:
No more, no less; enough to make me fear
The outcome cannot be good for our house.
Perhaps this is some demigod, the son
Of god or goddess whose displeasure we
Cannot assume. And he, a hero like
Proud Akhilleus on the windy plains
Of Ileum: unmatched by friend or foe.
Your wife am I, and happy, yet I'm sure
No joy as widow shall I ever know.
ODYSSEUS: So many men at arms have sought my measure!
Yet never did I run away in fear.
You named great Akhilleus, Thetis' son
Yet he lies dead in Troy, slain by a man.
While I, confronted by that one-eyed monster,
The mighty Kyclops humbled and escaped.
Would you have bade me cringe from him in fear
And begged for life, when he had slain my men?
I kept my courage 'gainst Poseidon's son,
And cannot now show fear against a man
Nor ask some others to provide relief
Against his blade.
PENELOPE: Behold your very words!
Brave Hector took the field and nobly led

The Trojan host until at length he fell
Where Akhilleus slew him. And that son
Of Thetis, confident against the world
At arms, yes even he would soon lie dead,
The conquest of a lesser man than he.
Until they fell, they never had known death
And always triumphed, always did prevail.
ODYSSEUS: And if it is my turn to taste defeat
I bid it welcome. Yet Dodona's words
From Zeus himself were clear: I shall not fall
Save at the hands of mine own son. So what
Have I to fear from this strange man?
I've heard your pleas; they fall upon deaf ears.
I shall away.
              [*Exit Odysseus*]

PENELOPE: If you must go, my son
Will now return. I shall the rowers summon
To bring him from that isle, once you depart
For I fear something dreadful in my heart
              [*Exit Penelope*]

STASIMON TWO

CHORUS [all]: What stranger comes to Ithaca's shores, well-arm'd
Intent to do us harm? What man is this
And of what sort, that he should take up arms
Against our kinsmen?
[First Four]: Who would dare invade?
Is this but one, or is he first of many?
[Second Four]: Is this in fact a man? Could he not be
Some god in mortal outfit? And if so,
Could this Poseidon be, intent to take
His vengeance 'pon old Laertes' proud son?
[Third Four]: And yet I have my doubts! A man half-drowned
Is not a god at all! He was attacked
By some, and vanquished some. Yet those he fought

Were farmers, not men trained in use of arms.
And why they fell upon him is unclear.
Some friend lay slain, and yet to blame his death
On one half-drowned, still wet and short of breath
Is folly.
[Fourth Four]: Yet another fear arises:
This was no stranger to our land at all
Perhaps, but Telemachus come to slay
His sire, and fulfill Dodona's curse.
[First Four]: This cannot be. For those two ships
Had not yet reached the rocky crag on which
He is condemned to exile, ere our foe
Upon our shores arrived. Therefore rejoice:
CHORUS [all]: Odysseus our great king cannot be slain
By any save Telemachus, and he
Was surely gone and left behind no traces
Unless he can at once be in two places!

EPISODE THREE

Enter TELEGONUS

CHORUS: But what is he who now intrudes upon us?
Speak, stranger, and state the reason wherefore
You come upon us, armed with fearful spear!
Your name, proud warrior?
TELEGONUS: Of no concern
At present; all will soon be told, but first
I beg you for your help. Your own great king
Lies wounded in the fields and in great pain,
His agony most dreadful to behold.
Through no design or wish to do him harm
But by some accident I fear I have
Upon him caused some scratch, through which, alas,
Some poison worse than serpent's bite has stung
And entered.
LEADER: Go, some four of you. Make haste,

And bring back to our palace him who rules.
[Exeunt Second Four]
And now, young warrior, you must tell your tale.
How came our king to suffer at your hands?
TELEGONUS: I shall reply, yet cannot tell you all
As I know not the shores 'pon which I've landed.
With two-score men at oars, I had embarked
Upon a mission on the wine-dark seas
And made good progress till the dark clouds rose
And cast a storm that sent us up and down
In terror that we'd lie in watery graves.
We could not see, save when a lightning bolt
From Zeus above struck near. Then all went black.
At length we heard a crash; the boat itself
Was dashed upon some rocks and quickly splintered.
I know not what befell my forty men,
Yet fear the worst. But for myself, I was
Perhaps more fortunate. Clutching my spear,
I leapt into the brine, where I soon found
A fragment, large and strong, from our doomed ship
And clutching this in one arm, I survived.
Then ceased the storm, and Phoebus' chariot
Brought forth the light of day. And to the west
I saw some beaches near enough to swim
And reached these shores. I soon heard human speech
I recognized as not unlike my own
And thanked the gods, quite confident I would
Be given hospitality by those
Whose lands I'd somehow reached. How wrong I was!
I had not yet cleared all Poseidon's seas
From out my ears when several men swooped down,
Some clutching staves and blades. "He's there!" they shouted
"'Tis he who slew our friend." Thus they approached.
Still dripping wet, I stared them down, and said,

"I slew no man, but only now arrived
At these, your shores. How could I have brought down
A native son, when I have not yet touched
Your soil, and barely stand upon my feet,
Half-drowned?" I thought sufficient argument
To halt their charge, but I was quite mistaken.
Despite my words, they did attack, and I
Fought back. I slew no man, although I'm sure
I wounded two or three, and at the sight
Of blood, the rabble fled. Thus, I escaped
Yet not long after I was once again
Approached, this time by one, a mighty man
Who had the bearings of a king. I knew
At once this was a noble lord, perhaps
A favorite of the gods. His royal bearings
Shone forth right through the armor that he wore
And through the visor of his helmet, too.
I had no wish to fight him, but instead
Held up my spear in peaceful gesture, thus.
[The Chorus gasp!]
Alas, the ancient did not understand
And saw my stance as violent so he drew
His sword and did attack. My longer spear
Did parry, but by chance it also cut
Him with this spine. He quickly fell and cried
In agonizing pain. At once I fled
Toward this great palace easily seen from where
Our battle had occurred. I pray no harm
Has come upon so great a lord as he
Did seem to be. And yet I fear the worst
For poison's no great friend to any man
Who feels it.
LEADER: Brave you are to tell the truth
And have no fears. For none can now blame you

For misinterpretation by the king.
'Twas thus you held your spear, but in our lands
The gesture is a challenge to defend
In mortal strife. You did prevail but need
Not fear the worst, for our king's fate is cast
He shall die slain, but only his fair son
Can do that deed. Now come – I hear the men
I sent away return. 'Tis safest if
You hide behind us till we can explain
What we have learned and look to our king's wounds.
[Enter ODYSSEUS on a litter, carried by Second Four, who place it down. He cries out in pain, yet struggles to his feet, assisted and held by some of the Second Four.]
ODYSSEUS: Aieoww! This is no mere scratch, for lo: it seeps some
Poison into me, and hurls me down the abyss to
Timeless death! My citizens, behold! Here lies
In his dying agonies, the hero who fought so bravely
On the wind-swept plains of Troy. I survived the arrows of Paris,
The spear of Troilus, the fearful ax of great Sarpedon, the son of Zeus.
Nor could the sword-thrusts of mighty Hector,
Greatest of the Trojan host, direct me to the River Styx.
And having outlasted the Trojans some half-score years,
I journeyed upon the seas, where I escaped the clutches
Of Poseidon's son, the mighty Kyklops, whom I blinded,
And when I mocked him, he hurled boulders at our ships,
Yet once again no harm befell me. Yet now -- Aieoww!
A painful poison from a tiny wound has slain me. A scratch
Has done what sons of Zeus and Poseidon could not.
My curses upon the priestess of Dodona, who told me false:
Why have I sent in exile my noble son, my own
Telemachus, who never did me harm? Go call him back
At once, and hope I can live long enough to see him.
LEADER: He is already summoned, my King, and will

Soon arrive. But perhaps you are not slain?
ODYSSEUS: Foolish man. One who has known war,
As those who fought upon the windy plains of Ileum knew war,
Knows all too well when wounds are mortal.
I am slain – not by my son, but by a stranger.
And yet, as I struggle for breath, I see myself
In different light. I am poisoned by a scratch,
Even as great Herakles was consumed
By Deianeira's robe. So let me summon back
The curses I laid about the priestess. Perhaps she spoke the truth:
Divine Herakles, from his agonies, sought release,
And charged his son, the noble Hyllus, to supply it:
Upon the pyre he laid his great father, and then applied the flame.
Thus did the hero die. I see it now: that my own agonies
Must last until Telemachus arrives and ends them.
And this, my friends, was what the Oracle meant,
Though we knew it not. I must die at the hands of my son,
But I must bless him for the kindness. Instead, foolishly,
I looked upon him as a foe, and instrument
Of my destruction. How soon will he be here,
That I may die?

The CHORUS are silent. At length:

LEADER: He will be here soon, I am sure.

CHORUS remain silent. ODYSSEUS moans, then screams, and then looks up at them.

ODYSSEUS: Why are you so silent? If you would tell me something
Do so quickly, for I have not long to live.

LEADER: My Lord – He who slew you does lament the accident
and begs your forgiveness.

TELEGONUS approaches. He and ODYSSEUS face each other. Suddenly, they sense some recognition.

ODYSSEUS: The fever sets upon me, yet I'd swear
I see within your features one I knew

And loved – a goddess true, who ruled an isle.
Her name was Kirke, and within your face
I see her nose, her chin, her sparkling eyes!
TELEGONUS: I am her son, and now I must confront
The saddest truth of all. Unless I'm wrong
This is Ithaca, and if you're its lord,
My sire as well. Are you --- Odysseus?
ODYSSEUS: The same, Laertes' son, and this land's king.
But now, I fear that once again I must
Against the priestess find myself corrected.
Behold! Through tragic accident my son
Has slain me. Oracles speak true, though we
Misunderstand them. Fools! That's what we are.
But come! My son, embrace your dying sire
That we may part in love.
TELEGONUS: Forgive me, please,
And know that when I held aloft this shaft
It was a sign in my homeland for truce.
For as you did descend upon the beach
Your face behind the helmet's visor hidden,
Yet by your stance, your stride, your noble bearing
I saw that which I knew: you were a king.
And had I known you were Odysseus,
I should more soon have ta'en this fearful shaft
And broken it upon my thigh before
I let it harm you. Still, when you attacked
I had no choice, and as your blow descended
I blocked it with my spear. Thus were you scratched.
[Enter TELEMACHUS, who approaches ODYSSEUS]
TELEMACHUS: My noble lord and father, still you live,
Although they say you are severely wounded.
What damage have you suffered? How came you here?
Why so short of breath, and why

Does the God of Fever set your skin afire?
ODYSSEUS (groans loudly, then shudders, and then looks up): My son,
   My noble first-born, Telemachus
   Who saved my life three times when we four
   Overpowered the vile suitors: Come! Accept my blessings.
   I was --- so wrong! It was not you who slew me,
   But 'twas indeed a son I never knew!
   [They both look at TELEGONUS.]
   I pray you forgive me first; I should not have exiled you.
   And then, I beg you look upon this man, this Telegonus,
   not as your enemy, but rather as your own brother
   Upon whom you can never seek revenge.
TELEMACHUS: I shall do as commanded. [Embraces TELEGONUS.]
   LEADER: How sad it is that brothers
   Should in this manner meet!
ODYSSEUS: This is a tale contrived by those above
   To whom we are at most dim-witted toys.
   Brave Telegonus whom I call my son
   Take Telemachus in, and let him know
   How all this came to pass. And while within
   Prepare my death-bed and call out my wife,
   Penelope, whom I must bid farewell.
[Exeunt TELEMACHUS and TELEGONUS. As Odysseus cries out in pain, enter PENELOPE.]
   PENELOPE [weeping]: Oh woe, Odysseus! I waited twenty years
   For your return. And yet, no sooner had we settled
   Back into our married lives, than off you sailed again,
   Carrying that oar upon your shoulders: some mission
   To appease Poseidon. This done, you sought more knowledge,
   And finding it within the Oracle's cave,
   You exiled Telemachus, only to die at the other's hands.
   [Enter TELEGONUS]

ODYSSEUS: It was you, wife, who offered me correction,
And taught me rightly, "Feeble are the wits
Of men." And yet, perhaps my pride itself
Led to my fall, for while you were most true
I had a son by Kirke. Thus, you see
I cannot blame another for my lapse:
I had two sons, and sought defense from one.
But let us note once more an adage true:
That feeble are the wits of men when paired
Against the gods! How true, and yes, how sad
I could not learn this truth until my death.
And like a fool, I sought to stay the will
The fates decreed!
TELEGONUS: Oh, my father!
I must share one more truth with you!
This spear, which brought you low, was never
Made by mortal hands. It is a weapon forged
In the fires by divine Hephaestus, a gift to
Kirke, my mother. And behold this barb:
A sting-ray's spine. 'Twas from this point
The poison came, so swiftly, from just the slightest scratch.
[Odysseus turns sharply: a painful realization sets in.]
This is the magic of the spear: that while I wield it
None can overcome me, for so the grey-eyed goddess,
Athena herself, promised my mother. A man has slain
Odysseus, but only armed with magic from the gods!
ODYSSEUS (growing weaker): Again I see more errors!
Tiresias, that all-knowing seer, had rightly warned me long ago
My death would come "out of the sea," because I had offended
Poseidon, lord of those watery realms. And here
I see the truth: the sting-ray's spine,
Brought from the sea, now leads me to the funeral pyre,
And even the grey-eyed daughter of Zeus
Conspires to lay me low, a victim of my mortal pride.

Come! Penelope and Telegonus, and some of you
Help me to within. The poison burns; the fever rages.
I have not long. Within the tree, whose roots lie deep
In that foundation: there do rest my head,
And let me die upon that wedding bed.
[Exeunt Odysseus, Penelope, Telegonus, and two of the Second Four. The latter soon return.]

STASIMON 3

CHORUS: How little man can ever hope to know
Or understand that fate the gods above
Have destined for him.
[First Eight]: Hark! I hear him scream
In darkest agony. What dreadful pains
The hero does convey.
[Second Eight]: How doubly sad
That he must suffer so before he dies
And like a woman wail as never did
Our king at Troy. But soft you now and listen:
[First Eight]: I hear no cries; perhaps he rests or sleeps.
[Second Eight]: No sounds – but lo! I hear great wailing now.
And fear the worst.

[Pause on stage.]

LEADER: Good friends, our noble lord
Odysseus has died. Once deemed the wisest
Of men, he set his wits against the gods'.
This lesson teaches well: the cleverest man
Could not escape his fate, slain by his son.
And by a weapon of the god he had
Offended, thus his pride was now brought low.
[Second Eight]: And afterward? Will Telemachus rule
As did his sire? And how of him who slew
Unwittingly, Telegonus, his son
Through Kirke?
[First Eight]: She who is divine can bring

A resolution to this misery:
'Tis simple: She can make them all divine
And marry Telemachus while her son
Can wed his sire's wife, Penelope.
Thus can the gods all sorrows wipe away
With twice the joys from doubled wedding day!
[The Chorus remain on stage, but withdraw to the rear.]

EXODOS

[Enter KIRKE]

KIRKE: And so they would believe!
Alas, not even the greatest of the Olympians –
To say far less of so minor a deity as I –
Can go beyond what Fate decrees. And had I power
To grant the joyous resolution of this play,
I would not do as they suggest. Though still, why halt
The songs of poets who tell such tales?
But know ye this: Although divine, I truly loved
A mortal hero, and did bear his son.
Still, when the grey-eyed daughter of great Zeus
Revealed what would transpire, then I knew
Odysseus was doomed. Poseidon, she, and Zeus
Himself decreed it. I had to play my role,
And ask Hephaestus for a spear, with Poseidon's
Poison in it. Once it was made, he never stood a chance.
Now send the noble hero on his way,
And let a goddess mourn his final day.
[Exeunt Kirke and Chorus, severally.]

THE END

About the Author

Lenny Cavallaro is a "Renaissance man" steeped in the classics: Greek tragedy, Shakespearean drama, and classical music. He has also boxed, earned a third-degree black belt in karate, refereed futsal and soccer, run marathons, and practiced hypnosis and reiki professionally.

Cavallaro is the author of *Trojan Dialogues: The Memoirs of Diomedes* and *The Greatest Champion Who Never Was*. Earlier in 2022, White Bird Publications released the first two novels of his series, *The Passion of Elena Bianchi*: *If Music Be the Food of Love* (January) and *Paradise Regained and Lost Again* (May).

Cavallaro has also recently completed *Sherlock Holmes and the Mysteries of the Chess World*, which Russell Enterprises will release in October. He also "edited and revised" *Paganini Agitato*, a novel by Ann Abelson, which Fomite Press has slated for release this fall.

An accomplished pianist and composer, Cavallaro performed Bach's *Six Partitas* to the highest critical acclaim in Carnegie Recital Hall and achieved even more recognition as a composer. Eleven volumes of his music have been published to date, and in 2015, he wrote a conjectural "completion" of Contrapunctus XIV from Bach's unfinished masterpiece, *The Art of the Fugue*.

www.ingramcontent.com/pod-product-compliance
Lightning Source LLC
Chambersburg PA
CBHW070441010526
44118CB00014B/2142